D1455904

ENDANGERED!

CROCODILES AND ALLIGATORS

Karen Haywood

Marshall Cavendish
Benchmark

New York

Marshall Cavendish Benchmark
99 White Plains Road
Tarrytown, New York 10591
www.marshallcavendish.us

All websites were available and accurate when this book was sent to press.

Editor: Peter Mavrikis
Publisher: Michelle Bisson
Art Director: Anahid Hamparian
Series Designer: Elynn Cohen
Cover Design by Kay Petronio

Library of Congress Cataloging-in-Publication Data

Haywood, Karen.
Crocodiles and alligators / by Karen Haywood.
p. cm. — (Endangered!)
Includes bibliographical references and index.
Summary: "Describes the characteristics, behaviors, and plights of
endangered crocodiles and alligators, and what people can do to
help"—Provided by publisher.
ISBN 978-0-7614-4048-2
1. Crocodiles—Juvenile literature. 2. Alligators—Juvenile literature.
I. Title.
QL666.C925H39 2011
597.98—dc22
2009020336

Front cover: Close-up of a crocodile, Spencer Creek Crocodile Ranch, Zimbabwe
Title page: An American alligator on a log
Back cover: Swimming saltwater crocodile (top); Black caiman and Butterfly, Pantanal, Brazil (bottom)
Photo research by Paulee Kestin

The photographs in this book are used by permission and through the courtesy of:
Alamy: Melvyn Longhurs, 14; rgbstudio, 28; David Pearson, 42; Arco Images GmbH, (back cover bottom);
Arnold: Peter Arnold/Photo Library, 4, 17, 43; Corbis: Tobias Bernhard, 36, (back cover top); © Visuals Unlimited/
Corbis, 39; Getty: Nancy Nehring, 8; Klaus Nigge/National Geographic, 13; Minden: Anup Shah/ npl/
Minden Pictures, 32; NGS: RICHARD NOWITZ, 1; CLAUS MEYER/MINDEN PICTURES, 10; Photo
Researchers: Suzanne L. & Joseph T. Collins, 15; Nature's Images, 18; Aaron Ferster, 40; Visuals Unlimited:
Brandon Cole, 20; Fritz Polking, 22, 24, 30; Ken Lucas, 27; Reinhard Dirscherl, 34.

Printed in Malaysia (T)
1 2 3 4 5 6

Contents

Crocodile or Alligator?

"What is the difference between crocodiles and alligators?" This seems to be the first question asked when the subject of alligators and crocodiles comes up in conversation. There are many differences, such as width of the **snout**, but also there are certain basic similarities. Crocodilians—which include alligators, caimans, crocodiles,

Whether a crocodile or an alligator, these creatures are a fearsome sight as they lurk in the water waiting for prey.

and gharials—are among the oldest surviving creatures on earth.

Scientists believe that the first crocodilians appeared more than 210 million years ago. Scientists called **paleontologists** have studied the fossil remains of an ancient crocodilian that lived 110 million years ago in Africa. This massive animal was the size of a school bus, which is why scientists nicknamed it SuperCroc. This species of crocodilian grew to 40 feet (12 meters) long and weighed as much as 17,500 pounds (8 metric tons). Its jaws were nearly 6 feet (1.8 m) long and held more than one hundred teeth. Though crocodilians the size of SuperCroc no longer exist, their smaller descendants are still living.

Today there are twenty-three **species**, or specific types, of crocodilians. Because they are **reptiles**, they are cold-blooded animals. This means that their body temperature is controlled by the temperature of their environment. (Mammals and other warm-blooded animals are able to control their own internal, or inside, temperatures.) When you see an alligator or crocodile basking in the sun, it is not simply resting. It is catching the sun's rays to warm its body and raise its body temperature. When it starts to get too hot for comfort, it takes off for the shade.

Because the environment controls the crocodilians' body temperatures, their **range**, or area where they live, is determined by climate. They live in warm regions where the temperature does not get too cold. They cannot live anywhere where there is not enough sun to warm them or shade or water to cool them.

Unlike humans, who are **omnivorous**, all crocodilians are **carnivorous**, which means they eat only meat. The Indian gharial's meat is mostly seafood, but all other crocodilians will hunt for all types of animal and reptilian **prey**.

We know a lot about crocodilians today because of the science called **herpetology**, which is the study of reptiles and amphibians. Herpetologists look at reptiles and **amphibians** from all angles. They study how and where the animals live. These scientists also track changes in animal populations and how changes in their environments—whether natural or caused by humans—affect the lives these animals live.

1

Alligators

Alligatorinae is a subfamily of the family *Crocodylidae* and consists of eight species. Two of these species are alligators, six are caimans. The snout of an alligator is different from both a crocodile and a caiman: it is broad and flat.

In the past the American alligator was hunted almost to extinction, but now it thrives in the swamps and wetlands of the southern United States.

AMERICAN ALLIGATOR

The American alligator likes to live in all kinds of sunny, watery homes: freshwater swamps, overgrown ponds, lakes, bayous, rivers, and streams. Their range covers from eastern North Carolina, south through South Carolina, Georgia, Florida, Alabama, Mississippi, Louisiana, to the Rio Grande in Texas, and up the Mississippi, Arkansas, and Red rivers to Arkansas and Oklahoma.

Although they prefer water, they can survive dry periods by digging holes in areas with tall grasses and reeds

Since they are reptiles, these American alligators are catching the sun's rays to raise the temperature of their bodies to get warm.

that protect them from too much sunlight. They survive cold, below freezing, weather in the northern regions of their range for short periods of time by lying in shallow water and sticking their nostrils up through the thin ice. Their long snout with nostrils at the end that point upward lets them breathe while the rest of the body is underwater. American alligators are one of the few species of crocodilians that can survive such cold temperatures.

An adult female American alligator averages 8.2 feet (2.5 m) long, while the average length for a male is 11.2 feet (3.4 m). Some very large males may reach a weight of 1,000 pounds (455 kilograms). Evidence from fossils shows that in ancient eras, the *Alligator mississippiensis* were as much as 20 feet (6 m) long!

This alligator has a lizardlike body with a muscular, flat tail and powerful jaws. The skin on its back is covered with bony plates called **osteoderms** and scales, or **scutes**, which look like, and actually serve as armor, or thick protection. Adults have dark stripes on the tail, while young alligators have bright yellow ones.

The American alligator's diet includes clams, shrimp,

In the 1500s Spanish sailors visiting the Americas thought the strange-looking alligator was a giant lizard. In Spanish *el lagarto* means "the lizard." English sailors thought they were saying *allagarter,* and over time it became *alligator.*

frogs, snakes, salamanders, fish, water birds, turtles, small mammals that come to the water's edge, and **carrion**—basically, anything that swims, crawls, flies, or walks! They will also rob nests and eat the eggs of geese and other waterfowl. They use their sharp teeth to seize and hold their victims. While small prey is swallowed whole, they shake large prey into smaller, manageable pieces. If it is very large, crocodilians bite it, then spin on the long axis of their bodies to tear off easily swallowed pieces.

It is very important that you keep yourself and your pets away from any water that may contain an alligator! Alligators have been known to attack children and even adults, probably because they think the human

The skin on the back of the alligator is covered with bony plates called osteoderms or scutes, which serve as protection.

is their usual, smaller prey, or because they are aggravated or provoked. Do not feed an alligator in the wild. It is extremely dangerous because it encourages alligators to approach humans for food. You really do not want to get too close to the seventy-four to eighty teeth that alligator has. If a tooth is lost or wears down, its replacement grows in. An alligator can use between two to three thousand teeth in a lifetime!

An American alligator can live about fifty years in

the wild. In the past it was almost hunted to **extinction** for its leather and meat, but laws against hunting have helped this reptile make a comeback. It is listed as threatened on the U.S. Endangered Species List. Where hunting is allowed, it is tightly controlled. The greatest threat to the American alligator now is loss of **habitat**, draining of wetlands for the building of houses and roads, and water pollution, especially by mercury and **dioxins**.

This Chinese alligator glides along the Yangtze River bank searching for food.

CHINESE ALLIGATOR

The Chinese alligator is one of the smaller crocodilian species. Adults range from 2 feet (61 centimeters) to 6 feet (1.8 m) long and may weigh up to 88 pounds (40 kg). It is different from the American alligator in other ways also. The end of its snout is slightly upturned and is more tapered—narrow at one end—than that of its American cousin. Its teeth are better at crushing hard shells because one of its preferred foods is mollusks (snails, clams, oysters). This alligator also eats insects, fish, young ducks and geese, and rodents.

During the cold, dry months of winter, Chinese alligators live in caves or burrows that they dig at the edges of wetlands. There they wait for spring, when they will spend

This tiny Chinese alligator is quite cute as a baby, though it's never to be cuddled.

their days soaking up the sunshine. As the hot weather of summer begins, they become more **nocturnal**.

The Chinese alligator, unlike its American cousin, is critically **endangered**. Its population has declined 80 percent in the past twenty years. The reason for the decline is mainly habitat destruction. The human population of China is currently over 1.3 billion, and it takes a great deal of land to grow enough food to feed that many people. Land where this reptilian used to live—the rivers, lakes, ponds, and marshlands of the Yangtze River region from Shanghai to Jianling and possibly into North Korea—is being converted into farmland and rice paddies. When farmers see an alligator, many kill it from fear or because they consider it a nuisance. Also, farmers put out poison for rats, and when the alligator eats the rats as prey, the poison also kills the alligator. Pollution and dam construction are also taking a toll on this rare animal.

CAIMANS

There are six caiman species of the subfamily *Alligatorinae* and the Black caiman is the largest. Male Black

Black caimans are the largest members of the subfamily Alligatorinae.

caimans can reach at least 13 feet (4 m) long, and 19 feet (5.8 m) caimans have been reported, but no official record exists. As its name announces, the skin of their back is black, but their belly is light and has no markings. The jaw is a yellowish brown. Unlike most crocodilians, the colors of the Black caiman remain sharp as it gets old. Since this animal grows to such great lengths, it also weighs a great deal, up to 1,000 pounds (454 kg).

Black caimans live in the Amazon River Basin of South America. It prefers stagnant lakes in the savanna. A savanna is a subtropical grassland that has few trees but plenty of swampy wetlands. When the lakes flood, the

The Black caiman is endangered today because of its skin, which makes attractive handbags, shoes, and belts.

caiman will migrate with the water of the flood to swamps and forests. Its diet includes fish such as piranhas and catfish and the capybara rodent, the largest of all living rodents, which can weigh more than 100 pounds (45 kg). The Black caiman, like many of its cousins, hunts for its food at night. It has very sharp eyesight and hearing.

Scientists believe that the Black caiman is a "keystone" species in its environment, meaning that many creatures depend on it for sustenance. It recycles **nutrients** to the bottom of the food chain, which is an important part of maintaining a healthy ecosystem. Fishermen say that when Black caimans disappear from a region, there are fewer fish to catch.

The Black caiman is endangered today because of its skin, which makes attractive leather products. Over the past one hundred years, hunting has slashed the population by an estimated 99 percent. A few management programs exist, but they focus on the legal protection of remaining wild populations. As with many other endangered animals, these laws are difficult to enforce.

2

Crocodiles

The fourteen species of crocodiles include twelve in the genus *Crocodylus*, one in genus *Osteolaemus*, and the false gharial, also known as the Tomistoma (*Tomistoma schlegelii*). Crocodiles are noticeably different from alligators in several ways. With the mouth closed, the large fourth tooth of the croc's lower jaw is clearly visible. The snout of the crocodile is narrower and longer than that of alligators and caimans, and the eyes are smaller and closer together.

The saltwater crocodile, the largest of all living reptiles, is fiercely dangerous.

AMERICAN CROCODILE

It may surprise you to know that south Florida is the only known place in the world where crocodiles and alligators live together in the same area. The American crocodile (*Crocodylus acutus*) also lives farther south in Mexico, Central America, the Greater Antilles—Cuba, Jamaica, Hispaniola, and Puerto Rico—and down to northern South

The powerful jaws of the American crocodile contain sixty-six to sixty-eight teeth, and this croc has taken very good care of his!

America. This crocodile has been endangered in Florida for many years, with the population today at fewer than nine hundred animals.

The American crocodile is happy in both freshwater (rivers, lakes, and reservoirs) and brackish coastal habitats (tidal estuaries, coastal lagoons, and mangrove swamps). They dig tunnels in river and lagoon embankments where they can escape from predators (humans) or from the extreme heat of the sun. There is a large population in the saltwater Lago Enriquillo in the Dominican Republic. This crocodile has salt glands in its tongue, which help it regulate the salinity—amount of salt—in its blood.

A most unusual location this population calls home is the 53 miles (85.3 kilometers) of cooling canals at the Turkey Point nuclear power plant on Biscayne Bay in Florida. The workers at the plant protect the crocodiles and count their nests each year to record population changes. The power plant is committed to protecting the American crocodile on their 12,700 acre (5,140 hect-ares) site.

When young, this crocodile is a light olive color with

thirteen to fifteen black stripes around its body. As it grows older, its color changes to dark olive or gray. One of the larger crocodilian species, adults grow to an average 13 feet (4 m) long. On rare occasions they may grow to 22 feet long (7 m). Their powerful jaws contain sixty-six

Close-up of the American crocodile's sharp teeth.

to sixty-eight teeth, which help it to live a good long time, up to seventy years! They prefer to dine at night on fish, turtles, birds, crabs, and mammals. Now and then a pet or farm animal will also serve as this crocodile's dinner.

Female American crocodiles build their nests by digging holes in the ground, unless they live in an area where a hole will flood. In that case, the future mother will build a mound out of plant matter. Nesting occurs following her courtship with a male that could last up to two months. She then lays her nest of eggs, sometimes as many as sixty, but normally between thirty-five and forty. The eggs usually hatch after ninety days.

The decline of the American crocodile population is due mainly to hunting for their skin, which is of a very high quality and was prized for making leather goods (boots, belts, purses) during the early twentieth century. It is also due to the loss of habitat—in particular, the destruction of coastal mangroves in Ecuador and the mangrove swamps at the edges of Everglades National Park in Florida.

In order to preserve the American crocodile, its home countries in North, Central, and South America must develop programs and enact laws restricting hunting and the destruction of its watery habitat.

CUBAN CROCODILE

This crocodile gets its name from the island where it lives, Cuba, which is south of Florida and west of Haiti in the Caribbean Sea. It lives only on a small portion of Cuba, in the Zapata Swamp in the northwest and in the Lanier Swamp on the Isle of Youth off the southwest coast. In the past, before this species was hunted to near extinction, it also lived in the Cayman and Bahama islands. Although it lives very near the ocean, this crocodile prefers freshwater swamps and marshes to saltwater beaches, much like the environment of Florida's Everglades.

While the Cuban crocodile can grow as large as 13 to 16 feet (4 to 5 m) long, the average length is around 9 feet (3 m). It has a yellow and black pattern on its back that has earned it the nickname "pearly" crocodile. The scales on its legs are quite large.

The Cuban crocodile has a pointed snout and a bulky, muscular body. It is aggressive, does not always flee when

The Cuban crocodile has stout, muscular legs that help it run fast on land.

attacked, and is highly defensive. On its head are bony ridges behind each eye that look like raised eyebrows or long, sloping horns. Its legs are short but very strong. While they are good swimmers in the water, they are also skillful runners on land. When it walks, its belly rarely touches the ground because its strong legs hold it up. It is known for leaping high out of the water, with a push from its powerful tail, to snatch prey from overhanging tree limbs.

When the female is ready to lay her eggs, she will either dig a hole for her nest or construct a mound from

The Zapata and Lanier swamps where most Cuban crocodiles live are very similar to the Florida Everglades.

sand and plant matter. The method she chooses depends on the availability of appropriate nesting material. The normal clutch size is between thirty and forty eggs.

Scientists believe that only three thousand to six thousand Cuban crocodiles remain in the wild because of hunting, habitat destruction, and the introduction by humans of the *Caiman crocodilus* (Spectacled caiman) into its Lanier swamp home. Another cause of its near extinction is its being "hybridized" through crossbreeding with the American crocodile. For these reasons it is listed as endangered on the **IUCN** Red List. The answer to the survival of the Cuban crocodile may unfortunately lie in breeding the species in captivity, which many zoos are trying to do.

NILE CROCODILE

The Nile crocodile has been written about in many works of fiction. Peter Pan flung Captain Hook's arm to a crocodile that liked it so much it followed him "ever since, from sea to sea and from land to land, licking its lips for the rest of me."

As its name suggests, the Nile crocodile lives in Africa, though not only near the Nile River. Its range extends from Sudan in the north all the way down to South Africa and across to Senegal on the Atlantic coast. In the past, this crocodile lived all across Africa, up through Egypt and into Israel and Palestine, but hunting and the construction of the Aswan dams in Egypt have reduced the

A Nile crocodile munches on lunch in the noonday sun.

populations. Some observers believe, however, that crocodiles are living again in some areas of Egypt.

A large crocodile, the Nile can grow up to 16 to 19 feet (5 to 6 m) long and weigh as much as 1,650 pounds (748 kg), but the average is 500 pounds (227 kg). Most Nile crocodiles are dark olive in color with a white belly.

The Nile crocodile eats mainly fish, but while hunting at night they will attack just about anything that comes to the water's edge to drink, whether it is a zebra, antelope, buffalo, small hippo, large cat, porcupine, birds, or even other crocodiles. It can eat up to half (250 pounds!) its body weight at one feeding. This crocodile has a reputation for being a man-eater, which is well deserved because they probably kill more people than all other crocodilian species combined. It is thought that as many as two hundred people each year die from the attack of a Nile crocodile.

Even though these crocodiles are fierce when hunting for food, both the male and female are very caring parents. After the female lays her eggs, both parents guard their nest ferociously until the eggs hatch. In fact, when it is close to the time for the eggs to hatch, they may roll

The diet of the Nile crocodile is mostly fish, and it can eat up to half its body weight at one feeding. When hungry, it will attack almost anything that crosses its path, including this unlucky wildebeest.

the eggs gently in their mouths to help the babies emerge from the shell. It is important to note that if the eggs are rolled over before they are ready to hatch, the **embryo** inside will die.

The white underside of this crocodile is greatly valued by hunters for the leather goods industry. During the 1940s through the 1960s, this crocodile was hunted nearly to extinction. Since that time, African as well as international laws and programs have helped in their return in many regions. Unfortunately, in some areas water pollution, hunting, and habitat loss due to wetlands draining and unchecked development have severely decreased this population.

SALTWATER CROCODILE

This is one of the few crocodiles that is not critically endangered, but it is interesting because it may be the largest reptile in the world and, as can be told by its name, it lives in saltwater, unlike its crocodilian cousins. This species has a far-reaching distribution, from the coast of southwestern India, Bangladesh, and Sri Lanka, as well as throughout most of Southeast Asia, including Vietnam, Myanmar (Burma), Thailand, Cambodia, Laos, and down to the Philippines, Malaysia, Indonesia, Papua New Guinea, Vanuatu, the Solomon Islands, and northern Australia.

Saltwater crocodiles wait quietly beneath the water for possible prey. Without warning they blast up from the water with a thrash of their tails and seize their victim.

In the past, the saltwater crocodile lived in Singapore and the Seychelles, too, but now is extinct there.

A colossally large animal, the saltwater crocodile can grow to 29.5 feet (9 m) long. One specimen that was killed in Bengal in the mid-nineteenth century measured 32.9 feet (10 m) long! That is about the length of a fire truck! Of course, most "salties" nowadays are smaller, averaging around 19 feet (6 m). It is not surprising, since they are such good swimmers, that their tail is longer than that of all other crocodilians. Its coloration, however, is typical for a crocodile—dark olive green to gray with a light belly.

In the wild, salties rest during the day, lying in the mud of a lagoon or lolling in shallow waters near the beach. When it is time to eat, the world is their oyster, which means they can have pretty much anything they want. When young, salties prefer food such as insects, amphibians, aquatic beetles, crustaceans, frogs, snakes, and fish. As they grow older and larger, they still eat small prey like mud crabs, turtles, snakes, and birds, but very large adults also may take down much larger prey, including monkeys, deer, buffalo, livestock, and even horses.

For the leather industry, the hide of a saltwater crocodile is the most valuable of any crocodile species. The skin of the belly has very small scales and a large area has no blemish-causing osteoderms, which means more

"Salties" are fine swimmers with extremely long, powerful tails.

products can be cut out from such perfect, unmarked skin. Hunting in the mid-twentieth century depleted much of this species throughout its range, but this has been controlled in some areas, particularly in Australia, and the animal is making a comeback. Poaching remains a problem, however, as does habitat destruction and killing by humans because of fear.

3

Gharials

There is only one living species of gharial and that is the *Gavialis gangeticus,* or the Indian gharial. The Indian gharial is a critically endangered species. The few remaining individuals can be found within the river systems of the Brahmaputra in Bhutan and India, the Indus in Pakistan, the Ganges in India and Nepal, and the Mahanadi in India, with other small populations in the Kaladan and the Irrawaddy rivers in Myanmar (Burma). This crocodilian

The last surviving species of the family Gavialidae, gharials have long, narrow snouts and live in deep rivers. These reptiles are critically endangered.

Gharials rarely leave the water, preferring to spend most of their lives in the river.

is **riverine**—it is suited to an aquatic lifestyle in the calm areas of deep, quickly moving rivers. It spends little time on land, doing so only to bask in the sun or to lay eggs in a sandy riverbank. Its short legs are not strong enough to carry it very far, so on land the Indian gharial slides on its belly.

The most distinctive looking of all crocodilians, the Indian gharial has a very long and narrow snout. As the male grows older, he develops a large growth on the end of his snout called a "ghara," which is Hindi for "pot," that is used in making sounds.

This species rivals the Nile crocodile for size as it, too, can grow up to 16 to 19 feet (5 to 6 m) long, and some scientists note it can reach over 26 feet (8 m). Young gharials are darkly blotched with dark bands, but as they grow older, they become dark olive on the top side with an ivory-colored belly.

Another distinction between other crocodilians and the Indian gharial is its diet. Juveniles eat insects and frogs, but as they grow older, their diet switches to fish. Most scientists believe that the gharial is a true **piscivore**, but others say that it will eat anything that floats by. It hunts—or rather, fishes—however, only for seafood.

Most sources agree that this gharial is in mortal danger as its wild populations are in serious decline. Their major threats in the early twenty-first century are habitat loss due to development and the disruption of populations

As the male gharial matures, he develops a large growth on the end of his snout called a ghara, which is Hindi for "pot." Apparently the lump resembles a cooking pot.

through fishing and hunting. These disturbances are so serious that the gharial is the first crocodilian to be recategorized as critically endangered on the 2007 IUCN Red List. The Gharial Multi-Task Force (GMTF) is a group of local and international crocodilian specialists spearheading an aggressive conservation effort to ensure that the Indian gharial does not disappear from the earth.

A herpetologist examining a young caiman. Herpetologists are scientists who study reptiles and amphibians.

SAVING CROCODILES AND ALLIGATORS

Of the twenty-three crocodilian species living on earth today, twelve need emergency conservation help. Loss of habitat due to the draining of swamps and wetlands and hunting for hides for leather goods have taken an enormous toll on these animals. Water pollution is yet another significant problem. Runoff from farms that contains fertilizers, **pesticides**, and veterinary medicines, as well as oil spills, industrial waste, garbage dumping, and many other pollutants harm all aquatic life, including crocodilians.

GLOSSARY

amphibians—A class of vertebrates.

carnivorous—Feeding on only animal meat.

carrion—The flesh of a dead animal, not killed as prey.

dioxin—A toxic hydrocarbon that occurs as a by-product of industry (such as papermaking) and the burning of waste.

embryo—The very young developing individual before birth.

endangered—Any species that is in danger of extinction throughout all or a significant portion of its range.

extinction—No longer active, living, or existing.

habitat—The typical environment where a plant or animal lives, grows, and reproduces.

herpetology—A division of zoology that focuses on reptiles and amphibians.

IUCN—International Union for Conservation of Nature, founded in 1948 as the world's first global environmental organization.

nocturnal—Occurring or active at night.

nutrients—The parts of foodstuff that nourish the body.

omnivorous—Feeding on both plants and animals.

osteoderm—Bony deposits that form the scales on the skin of reptilians.

paleontologist—A scientist who studies past ages through fossils.

pesticide—A poisonous substance used to destroy pests.

piscivore—A carnivorous animal that lives on eating fish.

poach—To hunt or fish unlawfully or to steal fish or game.

prey—Animals that are hunted and eaten by other animals as food.

range—The place where a certain kind of animal or plant naturally lives.

reptiles—Air-breathing vertebrates, such as alligators, crocodiles, snakes, lizards, and turtles, that moves on its belly or uses short legs, usually covered with scales.

riverine—Living on or near a river.

scute—A type of osteoderm that makes up the large, bony scales on a reptile's skin.

snout—A long, projecting nose.

species—A category of living things that ranks below a genus, and is made up of related individuals able to produce fertile offspring.

FIND OUT MORE

Books

Feigenbaum, Aaron. *American Alligators: Freshwater Survivors.* New York: Bearport Publishing, 2008.

Pringle, Laurence and Meryl Henderson. *Alligators and Crocodiles!: Strange and Wonderful.* Honesdale, PA: Boyds Mill Press, 2009.

Rushby, Pamela. *Discovering SuperCroc.* Washington, DC: National Geographic, 2007.

Web Sites

National Geographic
www.nationalgeographic.com/supercroc/exhibit.html

National Wildlife Federation. What Is a Green Hour?
www.greenhour.org

National Wildlife Federation. Wildlife Watch
www.nwf.org/kidzone

Nature. Critter Guide
www.pbs.org/wnet/nature/animals/alligator.html

St. Augustin Alligator Farm
www.alligatorfarm.com

INDEX

Pages numbers in **boldface** are illustrations.

ABOUT THE AUTHOR

Karen Haywood has edited and written many books for young readers. She lives in North Carolina where she watches the squirrels steal fruit from the apple trees in her backyard as she writes. Inspired by the first Earth Day in 1970, she has been a strong advocate for the environment and animal rights for many years.